SCOTT FORESMAN
READING STREET

KINDERGARTEN

COMMON CORE

Program Authors

Peter Afflerbach
Camille Blachowicz
Candy Dawson Boyd
Elena Izquierdo
Connie Juel
Edward Kame'enui
Donald Leu
Jeanne R. Paratore

P. David Pearson
Sam Sebesta
Deborah Simmons
Susan Watts Taffe
Alfred Tatum
Sharon Vaughn
Karen Kring Wixson

SAVVAS
LEARNING COMPANY

*We dedicate Reading Street to
Peter Jovanovich.*

*His wisdom, courage,
and passion for education
are an inspiration to us all.*

RENAISSANCE
Accelerated Reader

Copyright © 2013 by Savvas Learning Company LLC. All Rights Reserved. Printed in the United States of America.

This publication is protected by copyright, and permission should be obtained from the publisher prior to any prohibited reproduction, storage in a retrieval system, or transmission in any form or by any means, electronic, mechanical, photocopying, recording, or otherwise. For information regarding permissions, request forms, and the appropriate contacts within the Savvas Learning Company Rights Management group, please send your query to the address below.

Savvas Learning Company LLC, 15 East Midland Avenue, Paramus, NJ 07652

Attributions of third party content appear on page 144, which constitutes an extension of this copyright page.

Common Core State Standards: © Copyright 2010. National Governors Association Center for Best Practices and Council of Chief State School Officers. All rights reserved.

Savvas™ and **Savvas Learning Company™** are the exclusive trademarks of Savvas Learning Company LLC in the U.S. and other countries.

Savvas Learning Company publishes through its famous imprints **Prentice Hall**® and **Scott Foresman**® which are exclusive registered trademarks owned by Savvas Learning Company LLC in the U.S. and/or other countries.

Reading Street® and **Savvas Realize**™ are exclusive trademarks of Savvas Learning Company LLC in the U.S. and/or other countries.

Unless otherwise indicated herein, any third party trademarks that may appear in this work are the property of their respective owners, and any references to third party trademarks, logos, or other trade dress are for demonstrative or descriptive purposes only. Such references are not intended to imply any sponsorship, endorsement, authorization, or promotion of Savvas Learning Company products by the owners of such marks, or any relationship between the owner and Savvas Learning Company LLC or its authors, licensees, or distributors.

ISBN-13: 978-1-428-47359-1
ISBN-10: 1-428-47359-9

Dear Reader,

What do you think of Reading Street so far? You've learned lots of letters and sounds and words. Have AlphaBuddy and your *My Skills Buddy* helped you along the way?

On the next part of our trip, you will read about plants and animals, and there will be a special visit to a very large beanstalk.

So hop on board, and let's get going. There's lots more to learn.

Sincerely,
The Authors

Unit 2 Contents

Look at Us!

 How are animals and plants unique?

Week 1

Let's Listen for Initial Sounds 12

Comprehension: Compare and Contrast 14

Phonics and High-Frequency Words 16

I Can Read! Decodable Reader 7
  A Little Mat 18

Nonfiction • Science
Flowers by Vijaya Khisty Bodach
Big Book

Retell/Think, Talk, and Write 26

Let's Learn It! 28

Let's Practice It! Fable 30

4

Week 2

Let's Listen for Initial Sounds 32

Comprehension: Literary Elements 34

Phonics and High-Frequency Words 36

I Can Read! Decodable Reader 8
Sam and Tam 38

Big Book

Nonfiction • Science
Nature Spy by Shelley Rotner and Ken Kreisler

Retell/Think, Talk, and Write 46

Let's Learn It! 48

Let's Practice It! Fairy Tale 50

Unit 2 Contents

Week 3

Let's Listen for Initial Sounds 52

Comprehension: Main Idea 54

Phonics and High-Frequency Words 56

I Can Read! Decodable Reader 9

My Map 58

Nonfiction • Science
Animal Babies in Grasslands
by Jennifer Schofield

Retell/Think, Talk, and Write 66

Big Book

Let's Learn It! 68

Let's Practice It! Folk Tale 70

Week 4

Let's Listen for Initial Sounds 72

Comprehension: Realism and Fantasy 74

Phonics and High-Frequency Words 76

I Can Read! Decodable Reader 10

My Cap 78

Animal Fantasy • Science
Bear Snores On by Karma Wilson

Retell/Think, Talk, and Write 86

Big Book

Let's Learn It! 88

Let's Practice It! Lullaby 90

Week 5

Let's Listen for Initial Sounds 92

Comprehension: Sequence 94

Phonics and High-Frequency Words 96

I Can Read! Decodable Reader 11
   Tip and Pat 98

Nonfiction • Science
A Bed for the Winter by Karen Wallace

Big Book

Retell/Think, Talk, and Write 106

Let's Learn It! 108

Let's Practice It! Nursery Rhyme 110

Week 6

Let's Listen for Initial Sounds 112

Comprehension: Realism and Fantasy 114

Phonics and High-Frequency Words 116

I Can Read! Decodable Reader 12
   Tim and Sam 118

Fairy Tale • Social Studies
Jack and the Beanstalk
retold by Mary Ann Hoberman

Big Book

Retell/Think, Talk, and Write 126

Let's Learn It! 128

Let's Practice It! Expository Text 130

READING STREET The Digital Path!

Don Leu
The Internet Guy

Right before our eyes, the nature of reading and learning is changing. The Internet and other technologies create new opportunities, new solutions, and new literacies. New reading comprehension skills are required online. They are increasingly important to our students and our society.

Those of us on the Reading Street team are here to help you on this new, and very exciting, journey.

See It!

- Big Question Video

- Concept Talk Video

- Envision It! Animations

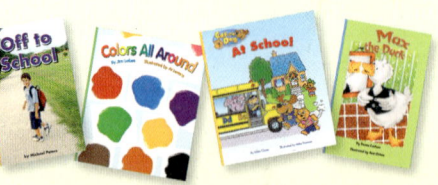

- eReaders

Hear It!

- Sing with Me Animations

- eSelections

- Grammar Jammer

Adam and Kim play at the beach.

Concept Talk Video

Do It!

- Story Sort 
- eReaders 
- Letter Tile Drag and Drop

Unit 2

Look at Us!

How are animals and plants unique?

Reading Street Online
www.ReadingStreet.com
- Big Question Video
- Envision It! Animations
- Story Sort

Phonemic Awareness

Let's Listen for

Initial Sounds

- Say *Ann, Al, Andy*. What sound do you hear at the beginning of these names?
- Find three things that begin with /a/, like *Ann*.
- Point to these pictures and say these words: *bed, pillow, rug*. Do they begin with the same sound? What about *ant, alligator, astronaut*?
- What rhymes with *Ann*?

READING STREET ONLINE
BIG QUESTION VIDEO
www.ReadingStreet.com

Common Core State Standards
Foundational Skills 2.d. Isolate and pronounce the initial, medial vowel, and final sounds (phonemes) in three-phoneme (consonant-vowel-consonant, or CVC) words. Also Foundational Skills 2.e.

Common Core State Standards
Informational Text 3. With prompting and support, describe the connection between two individuals, events, ideas, or pieces of information in a text.

Comprehension

Envision It!
Compare and Contrast

READING STREET ONLINE
ENVISION IT! ANIMATIONS
www.ReadingStreet.com

astronaut

Phonics
Short Aa

Words I Can Blend

High-Frequency Words

Words I Can Read

have

is

Sentences I Can Read

1. I have a mat.
2. The mat is little.
3. Tam is little.

Common Core State Standards
Foundational Skills 4. Read emergent-reader texts with purpose and understanding. Also Foundational Skills 3., 3.a., 3.c.

Phonics

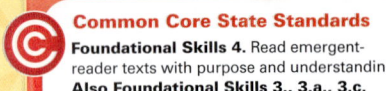

Decodable Reader

- Short *a*
  am
  Tam
  mat
  at

- High-Frequency Words
  I
  am
  is
  little
  have
  a
  the

▲ Read the story.

READING STREET ONLINE
DECODABLE eREADERS
www.ReadingStreet.com

A Little Mat

Written by Alex Altman
Illustrated by Mary Stern

Decodable Reader 7

I am Tam.

Is Tam little?

Tam is little.

I have a mat.

Is the mat little?

The mat is little.

Tam is at the mat.

Think, Talk, and Write

1. Tell about a unique flower you have seen. **Text to Self**

2. How are a rose and a cauliflower alike? How are they different?

Compare and Contrast

3. Look back and write.

Common Core State Standards

Speaking/Listening 2. Confirm understanding of a text read aloud or information presented orally or through other media by asking and answering questions about key details and requesting clarification if something is not understood. **Also Language 5.a., 6.**

Let's Learn It!

Vocabulary

- What do you see that is yellow?
- What do you see that is purple?
- What do you see that is orange?

Listening and Speaking

- What happens first in the story?
- What happens next in the story?
- What happens last in the story?

Vocabulary

Color Words

yellow

purple

orange

Listening and Speaking

Listen for Sequence

Be a good listener!

Common Core State Standards
Literature 1. With prompting and support, ask and answer questions about key details in a text. Also Literature 2., 5., 9.

Let's Practice It!

Fable

- Listen to the fable.
- How are the two characters different?
- What is the field like in summer? in winter?
- How is this story like "The Boy Who Cried Wolf!"?
- What new expression does this fable teach you?

The Ant and the Grasshopper

Common Core State Standards
Foundational Skills 2.d. Isolate and pronounce the initial, medial vowel, and final sounds (phonemes) in three-phoneme (consonant-vowel-consonant, or CVC) words. **Also Foundational Skills 2.a., 2.e.**

Phonemic Awareness

Let's Listen for

Initial Sounds

- Say *Sam*, *Seth*, *Sue*. What sound do you hear at the beginning of these names?

- Point to the sun. Find three things that begin with /s/, like *sun*.

- Point to these pictures and say the words: *table*, *soap*, *fork*. Do they begin the same? What about *salt*, *socks*, *silverware*?

- Which words rhyme? socks/clocks? Sam/Sally? Sue/you?

- What sounds might you hear in a school lunchroom?

READING STREET ONLINE
BIG QUESTION VIDEO
www.ReadingStreet.com

Common Core State Standards

Literature 3. With prompting and support, identify characters, settings, and major events in a story.

Comprehension

Envision It!
Literary Elements

READING STREET ONLINE
ENVISION IT! ANIMATIONS
www.ReadingStreet.com

Characters

Setting

34

Plot

Common Core State Standards
Foundational Skills 3.a. Demonstrate basic knowledge of one-to-one letter-sound correspondences by producing the primary or many of the most frequent sounds for each consonant.
Also Foundational Skills 2.d., 3.c.

Ss

salamander

**READING STREET ONLINE
ALPHABET CARDS**
www.ReadingStreet.com

Phonics

Initial Ss

Words I Can Blend

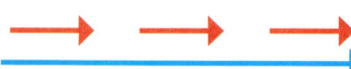

High-Frequency Words

Words I Can Read

have

is

Sentences I Can Read

1. I have Sam.
2. Sam is little.
3. Sam is a 🐱.

Phonics

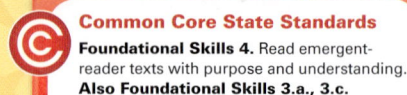

Decodable Reader

- Consonant *Ss*
  Sam
  sat

- High-Frequency Words
  I
  am
  have
  a
  the
  is

▲ Read the story.

READING STREET ONLINE
DECODABLE eREADERS
www.ReadingStreet.com

Sam and Tam

Written by Paul Thomas
Illustrated by Katie Snell

Decodable Reader 8

I am Sam.

I have a mat.

Sam sat at the mat.

I am Tam.

Tam is at the mat.

Tam sat at the mat.

Tam sat.
Sam sat.

Think, Talk, and Write

1. What did you learn about nature from the story?

   Text to Self

2. Where does *Nature Spy* take place?

   🎯 **Setting**

3. Look back and write.

Common Core State Standards
Speaking/Listening 1.a. Follow agreed-upon rules for discussions (e.g., listening to others and taking turns speaking about the topics and texts under discussion). Also Speaking/Listening 2., Language 5.a., 6.

Let's Learn It!

Vocabulary
- Talk about the pictures.
- What grows near your home?

Listening and Speaking
- Follow AlphaBuddy's directions.
- Act like an animal.

Vocabulary

Nature Words

flower

tree

leaf

grass

Listening and Speaking

Listen for Directions

Be a good listener!

Common Core State Standards
Literature 5. Recognize common types of texts (e.g., storybooks, poems).
Also Literature 1., 2.

Let's Practice It!

Fairy Tale

- Listen to the fairy tale.
- How can you tell this is a fairy tale?
- Why does the elf grant Josef three wishes?
- How do Josef and Anna waste two wishes?
- Tell why you think people like to read and listen to fairy tales.

The Three Wishes

50

Common Core State Standards
Foundational Skills 2.d. Isolate and pronounce the initial, medial vowel, and final sounds (phonemes) in three-phoneme (consonant-vowel-consonant, or CVC) words. **Also Foundational Skills 2.b., 2.e.**

Phonemic Awareness

Let's Listen for

Initial Sounds

- Say *Pat, Pam, Pete*. What sound do you hear at the beginning of these names?

- Find three things in the picture that begin like *Pat*.

- Point to these pictures and say the words: *paper, panda, penguin*. Do they begin the same? What about *pig, door, street*?

- Name a color you see in the picture. Clap the word parts. How many claps?

READING STREET ONLINE
BIG QUESTION VIDEO
www.ReadingStreet.com

52

Phonics

Initial and Final *Pp*

Words I Can Blend

P a m

m a p

P a t

t a p

m a t

High-Frequency Words

Words I Can Read

we

like

Sentences I Can Read

1. We have a map.
2. We like the map.
3. My map is little.

Common Core State Standards
Foundational Skills 4. Read emergent-reader texts with purpose and understanding. Also Foundational Skills 3.a., 3.c.

Phonics

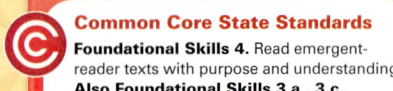

Decodable Reader

- Consonant *Pp*
  Pam
  map
  tap
  pat

- High-Frequency Words
  I   am
  have   a
  the   my
  we   like

▲ Read the story.

**READING STREET ONLINE
DECODABLE eREADERS**
www.ReadingStreet.com

My Map

Written by Jerry Moore
Illustrated by Chris Brown

I am Pam.

I have a map.

The map sat at the mat.

I tap my map.

We tap the map.

We pat at the map.

We like the map.

Think, Talk, and Write

1. How are most animal babies the same? *Text to World*

2. What is *Animal Babies in Grasslands* about?

🎯 Main Idea

3. Look back and write.

Common Core State Standards
Speaking/Listening 1.b. Continue a conversation through multiple exchanges.
Also Language 6.

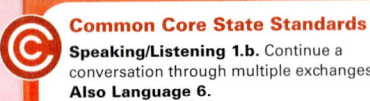

Vocabulary
- Talk about the pictures.
- Where do these animal babies live?

Listening and Speaking
- Say one thing about yourself.
- Listen to others talk about themselves.
- Retell facts about a friend.

Vocabulary

Words for Animal Babies

puppy

kitten

chick

calf

Listening and Speaking

Discussion

Be a good speaker!

Anansi's Hat Shaking Dance

Let's Practice It!

Folk Tale

- Listen to the folk tale.
- Where and when does the story take place?
- Why does Anansi put his hat back on?
- Tell about Anansi. What is he like?
- Share ideas about what you learn from Anansi that can help you.
- What questions do you have about this folk tale?

Common Core State Standards
Literature 1. With prompting and support, ask and answer questions about key details in a text. Also Literature 2., 3., 5.

Common Core State Standards
Foundational Skills 2.d. Isolate and pronounce the initial, medial vowel, and final sounds (phonemes) in three-phoneme (consonant-vowel-consonant, or CVC) words. **Also Foundational Skills 2.b.**

Phonemic Awareness

Let's Listen for

Initial Sounds

Read Together

- Say *Carl, Cam, Cate.* What sound do you hear at the beginning of these names?

- Point to the cart in the picture. Find three things that begin with /k/, like *cart.*

- Name other words that begin with /k/.

- Point to and say, *Carrots and cucumbers are in the cart.* What sound do you hear repeated?

- Say *cucumber.* Clap the word parts. How many claps?

READING STREET ONLINE
BIG QUESTION VIDEO
www.ReadingStreet.com

Common Core State Standards
Foundational Skills 3.a. Demonstrate basic knowledge of one-to-one letter-sound correspondences by producing the primary or many of the most frequent sounds for each consonant.
Also Foundational Skills 3.c., 3.d.

Phonics

Initial and Final *Cc*

Words I Can Blend

High-Frequency Words

Words I Can Read

we

my

like

Sentences I Can Read

1. I like Cam.
2. We like to sit.
3. We like my cat.

Common Core State Standards
Foundational Skills 4. Read emergent-reader texts with purpose and understanding. Also Foundational Skills 3.a., 3.c.

Phonics

Decodable Reader

- Consonant Cc
  Cam
  Mac
  cap

■ High-Frequency Words
  I   am
  we   have
  a   is
  the   my
  like

▲ Read the story.

READING STREET ONLINE
DECODABLE eREADERS
www.ReadingStreet.com

My Cap

Written by Sue Bear
Illustrated by Lori Burk

Decodable Reader 10

I am Cam.
I am Mac.

We have a cap.

Cam is at the cap.

Is the cap my cap?

Mac is at the cap.

Is the cap my cap?

I like my cap.

Think, Talk, and Write

1. What does a bear do in the winter? **Text to World**

2. Which story is about real animals? Which is about make-believe animals?

Realism and Fantasy

3. Look back and write.

Common Core State Standards

Literature 3. With prompting and support, identify characters, settings, and major events in a story. **Also Speaking/Listening 2., Language 6.**

Let's Learn It!

Vocabulary
- Talk about the pictures.
- Which season is your favorite?

Listening and Speaking
- Where do AlphaBuddy's stories take place?

Vocabulary

Words for Nature

spring

summer

fall winter

88

Listening and Speaking

Listen for Setting

Be a good listener!

Common Core State Standards
Foundational Skills 2.a. Recognize and produce rhyming words.
Also Literature 1., 3., 5.

Let's Practice It!

Lullaby

- Listen to the lullaby.
- Sing the lullaby. Sway in time to its rhythm.
- Which words in the lullaby rhyme?
- Who is often a main character in a lullaby? Why?
- Which part of the lullaby is make-believe?

Rock-a-Bye, Baby

Common Core State Standards
Foundational Skills 2.b. Count, pronounce, blend, and segment syllables in spoken words. **Also Foundational Skills 2.**

Phonemic Awareness

Let's Listen for

Initial Sounds

- Say *Isabel, Izzy, Inga*. What sound do you hear at the beginning of these names?

- Find three things that begin with /i/, like *Isabel*.

- Point to these pictures: *ink, iguana, igloo*. Do they begin the same? What about *insects, books, posters*?

- Say *inventor*. Clap the word parts. How many claps?

- What sounds would you hear in a library? What kind of voice should you use?

READING STREET ONLINE
BIG QUESTION VIDEO
www.ReadingStreet.com

Read Together

92

Common Core State Standards
Informational Text 3. With prompting and support, describe the connection between two individuals, events, ideas, or pieces of information in a text.

Comprehension

Envision It!
Sequence

**READING STREET ONLINE
ENVISION IT! ANIMATIONS**
www.ReadingStreet.com

94

Common Core State Standards
Foundational Skills 3. Know and apply grade-level phonics and word analysis skills in decoding words.
Also Foundational Skills 2.d., 3.a., 3.b., 3.c.

Phonics

Short *Ii*

Words I Can Blend

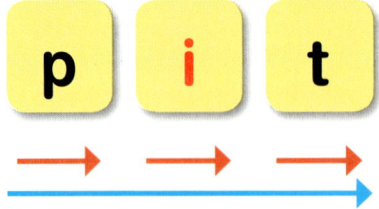

High-Frequency Words

Words I Can Read

he

for

Sentences I Can Read

1. He is a cat.
2. The cat is for Tim.
3. He can sit for Tim.

Common Core State Standards
Foundational Skills 4. Read emergent-reader texts with purpose and understanding. Also Foundational Skills 3., 3.a., 3.c.

Phonics

Decodable Reader

- Short *i*
  Tip
  it
  sit

- High-Frequency Words
  is
  a
  he
  my
  for

▲ Read the story.

**READING STREET ONLINE
DECODABLE eREADERS**
www.ReadingStreet.com

Tip and Pat

Written by Kate Brand
Illustrated by Carl Johnson

Decodable Reader 11

Tip is a cat.

He is my cat.

Pat is a cat.

He is my cat.

It is for Tip.

It is for Pat.

Sit, Tip, sit.
Sit, Pat, sit.

Think, Talk, and Write

1. Which bed reminded you of *Bear Snores On*? **Text to Text**

2. Where does the dormouse go first in the story? Where does she go last?

Sequence

3. Look back and write.

Common Core State Standards

Speaking/Listening 4. Describe familiar people, places, things, and events and, with prompting and support, provide additional detail. **Also Language 6.**

Let's Learn It!

Vocabulary

- Talk about the pictures.
- What do you do to get ready for school? Use sequence words.

Listening and Speaking

- What do the clocks look like?
- What do the dogs look like?

Vocabulary

Sequence Words

first

second

next

last

Listening and Speaking

Give a Description

Be a good speaker!

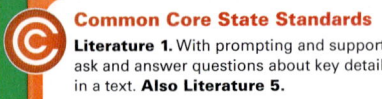

Common Core State Standards
Literature 1. With prompting and support, ask and answer questions about key details in a text. **Also Literature 5.**

The House That Jack Built

Let's Practice It!

Nursery Rhyme

- Listen to the rhyme.
- Recite the rhyme. Clap your hands to show the beats.
- How does Jack feel about his house? How can you tell?
- Tell about a time when it rained on you. Did you feel like these animals felt?

Common Core State Standards
Foundational Skills 2.d. Isolate and pronounce the initial, medial vowel, and final sounds (phonemes) in three-phoneme (consonant-vowel-consonant, or CVC) words.

Phonemic Awareness

Let's Listen for

Initial Sounds

- Say the sound you hear at the beginning of *in*, *ask*, *sign*, *pears*, *cast*.
- Point to the picture of *in*. Find a picture that begins with /i/, with /a/, with /s/, with /p/, with /k/.
- Name other words that begin with /i/, /a/, /s/, /p/, /k/.

**READING STREET ONLINE
BIG QUESTION VIDEO**
www.ReadingStreet.com

Common Core State Standards
Literature 5. Recognize common types of texts (e.g., storybooks, poems).

Comprehension

Envision It!

Realism and Fantasy

READING STREET ONLINE
ENVISION IT! ANIMATIONS
www.ReadingStreet.com

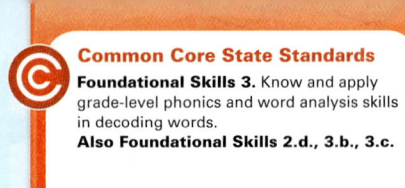

Phonics

Short *Ii*

Words I Can Blend

High-Frequency Words

Words I Can Read

he

for

Sentences I Can Read

1. He is my cat, Pip.
2. Pip can sit for Tim.
3. He can tap it.

Common Core State Standards
Foundational Skills 4. Read emergent-reader texts with purpose and understanding. Also Foundational Skills 2.d., 3., 3.c.

Phonics

Decodable Reader

- Short *i*
  sit
  Tim
  tip
  it

- High-Frequency Words
  I   am
  have   he
  is   my
  we   a
  for

▲ Read the story.

READING STREET ONLINE
DECODABLE eREADERS
www.ReadingStreet.com

Tim and Sam

Written by Joei Shavitz
Illustrated by Lawrence Paul

Decodable Reader 12

I am Sam.
I sit.

Tim sat.
I have Tim.

He is my cat.

I pat Tim.

We tip.

I am Sam.
I sit.

It is a mat for Tim.

Think, Talk, and Write

1. How are the plants in *Flowers* and *Jack and the Beanstalk* the same? How are they different? **Text to Text**

2. Which story is real?

Which is make-believe?

Realism and Fantasy

3. Look back and write.

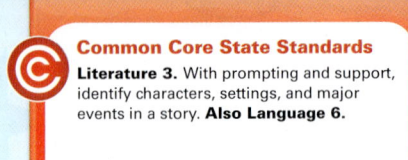

Common Core State Standards

Literature 3. With prompting and support, identify characters, settings, and major events in a story. **Also Language 6.**

Let's Learn It!

Vocabulary
- Talk about the picture.
- ■ Raise your right hand.
- ▲ Raise your left hand.

Listening and Speaking
- What happens in the story?

Vocabulary

Direction Words

left   right

Listening and Speaking

Listen for Plot

Be a good listener!

Common Core State Standards
Informational Text 7. With prompting and support, describe the relationship between illustrations and the text in which they appear (e.g., what person, place, thing, or idea in the text an illustration depicts).
Also Informational Text 1., 2.

Let's Practice It!

Expository Text

- Look at the title and the pictures. What will the selection be about?
- Listen to the selection.
- How do roots help a plant?
- Where are the leaves on a plant?
- What does the author tell about first? second? third? last?

Parts of a Plant

Leaf

Roots

130

Flower

Stem

131

Pictionary

Words for Things That Go

airplane

bike

truck

car

bus

van

boat

train

Words for Colors

Pictionary

Words for Shapes

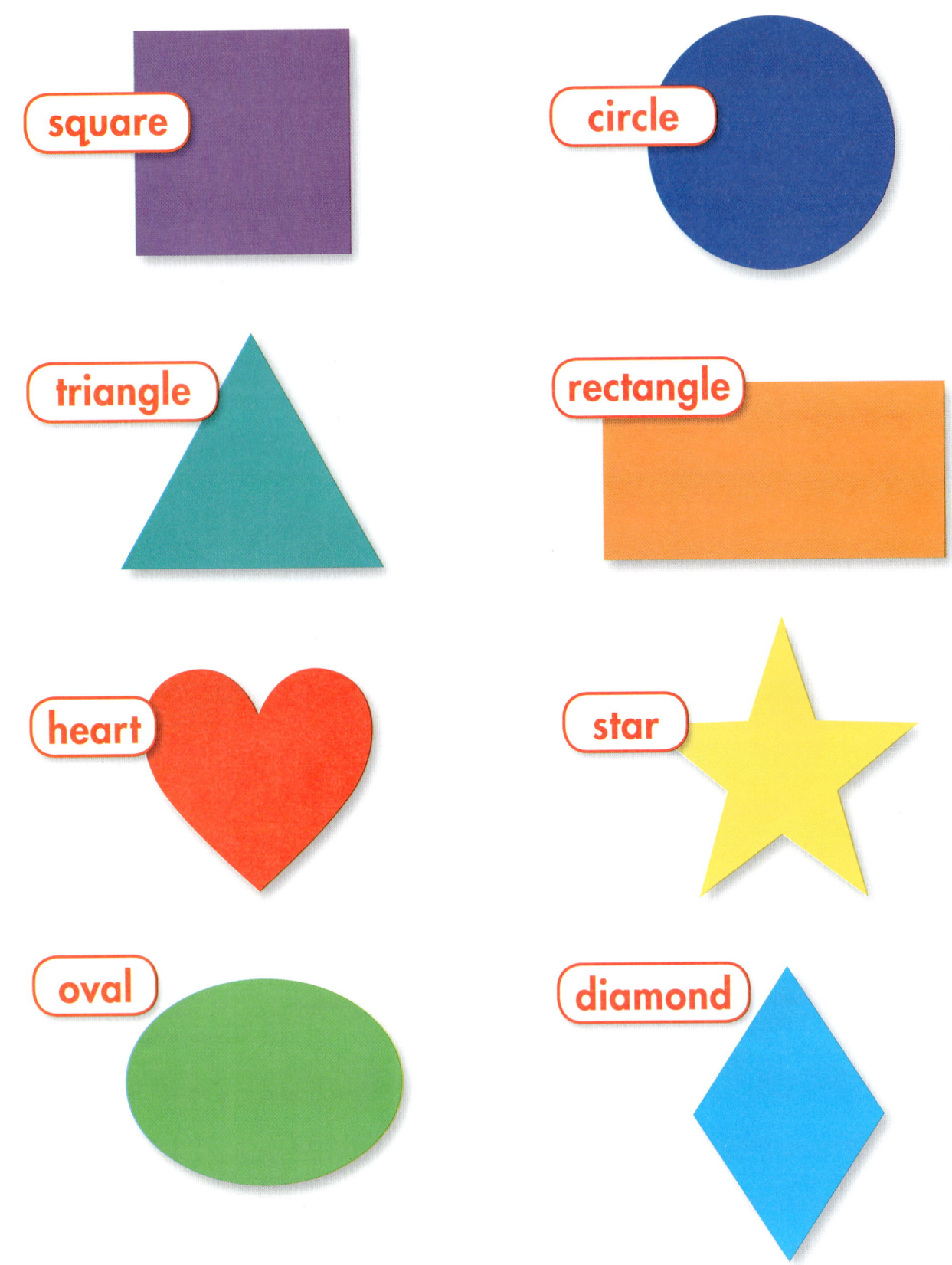

134

Words for Places

school

home

park

train station

police station

fire station

post office

library

butterfly

fish

whale

caterpillar

bear

panda

beaver

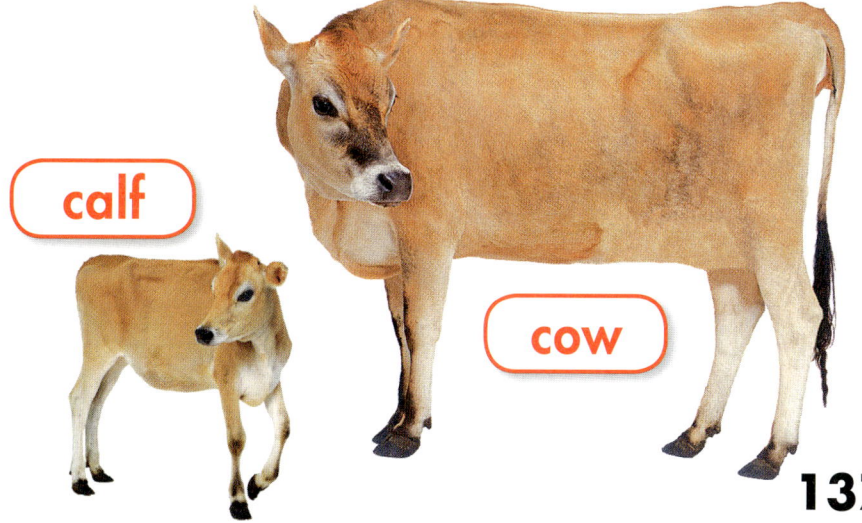
calf

cow

Pictionary

Words for Actions

skip

walk

run

fly

swim

ride

jump

hop

Position Words

Pictionary

My Classroom

Pictionary

Words for Feelings

happy

frightened

worried

excited

angry

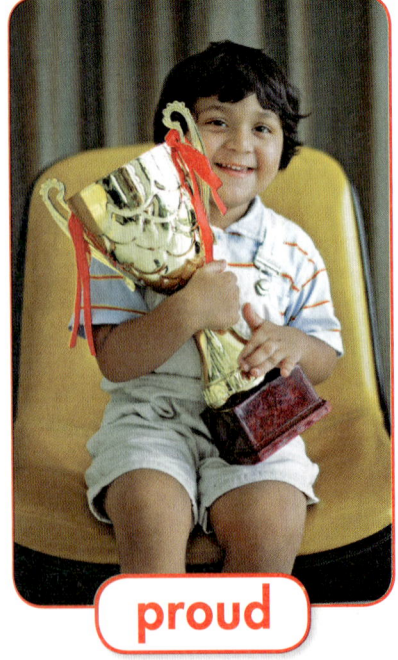
proud

sad

surprised

Acknowledgments

Illustrations
Cover: Rob Hefferan
12 Natalia Vasquez
28, 32, 48, 69, 88–89, 108–109 Mick Reid
30–31 Paul Meisel
50–51 Colleen Madden
52 Carolyn Croll
59–65 Maria Mola
70–71 Carolina Farias
72 Susan Mitchell
79–85 Wednesday Kirwan
90–91 David Austin Clar
92 Anthony Lewis
99–105 Cale Atkinson
110–111 Remy Simard
112 Jannie Ho
119–125 Robbie Short

Photographs
Photo locators denoted as follows: Top (T), Center (C), Bottom (B), Left (L), Right (R), Background (Bkgd)

10 (B) ©William Leaman/Alamy
16 GRIN/NASA
36 ©Sozaijiten/Savvas Learning Company
49 Cyril Laubscher/©DK Images, Dave King/©DK Images, Geoff Brightling/©DK Images, Mike Dunning/©DK Images
56 (TL) ©Jan Martin Will/Shutterstock
68 ©DK Images, Jane Burton/©DK Images
76 ©JLV Image Works/Fotolia
96 ©mario beauregard/Fotolia
116 ©mario beauregard/Fotolia
130 (T) ©DK Images
131 (T, B) ©DK Images
132 (CR) ©Basement Stock/Alamy, (TR, TL, TC, BL) Getty Images
133 (B) Getty Images
135 (BCL) ©Guillen Photography/Alamy Images, (BCR) ©Kinn Deacon/Alamy Images, (BR) Flavio Beltran/Shutterstock, (TCR) Photos to Go/Photolibrary
136 (BR) ©Arthur Morris/Corbis, (CC) ©Cyril Laubscher/DK Images, (TL) ©Dave King/DK Images, (BC) ©Gordon Clayton/DK Images, (CR) ©Karl Shone/DK Images, (CL) ©Marc Henrie/DK Images, (TR) DK Images, (TC, BCL) Getty Images, (BL) Jane Burton/(c)DK Images
137 (CR) ©A. Ramey/PhotoEdit, ©Comstock Images/Jupiter Images, (CL) ©Cyndy Black/Robert Harding World Imagery, (CC) ©Dave King/DK Images, (BR, BC) ©Gordon Clayton/DK Images, ©Rudi Von Briel/PhotoEdit, (TC, BL) Getty Images
138 (TR) ©Rubberball Productions, (BR) Jupiter Images, (TL) Photodisc/Thinkstock/Getty Images, (BC) Photos to Go/Photolibrary, (TC) Steve Shott/©DK Images
139 (TR, TC) ©Max Oppenheim/Getty Images, (CR, BR) Getty Images, (C, BL) Rubberball Productions
142 (CR) ©pete pahham/Fotolia, (BL) ©Simon Marcus/Corbis, (TR, TL) Getty Images, (TC) Jupiter Images, (C) Photos to Go/Photolibrary, (BR) Rubberball Productions